Meet Our New Student From

QUEBEC

Mitchell Lane

PUBLISHERS

P.O. Box 196

Hockessin, Delaware 19707

Visit us on the web: www.mitchelllane.com

Comments? email us: mitchelllane@mitchelllane.com

Ann Weil

Mitchell Lane
PUBLISHERS

Meet Our New Student From

Australia • China • Colombia • Great Britain
• Haiti • India • Israel • Japan • Korea • Malaysia •
Mali • Mexico • New Zealand • Nicaragua • Nigeria
• **Quebec** • South Africa • Tanzania • Zambia •
Going to School Around the World

Copyright © 2010 by Mitchell Lane Publishers

All rights reserved. No part of this book may be reproduced without written permission from the publisher. Printed and bound in the United States of America.

PUBLISHER'S NOTE: The facts on which the story in this book is based have been thoroughly researched. Documentation of such research can be found on page 44. While every possible effort has been made to ensure accuracy, the publisher will not assume liability for damages caused by inaccuracies in the data, and makes no warranty on the accuracy of the information contained herein.

Ce livre est dédié à Jéremy et sa famille. Merci! (This book is dedicated to Jéremy and his family. Thank you!)

**Library of Congress
Cataloging-in-Publication Data**
Weil, Ann.
  Meet our new student from Quebec / by Ann Weil.
    p. cm. — (Robbie reader. Meet our new student from . . .)
  Includes bibliographical references and index.
  ISBN 978-1-58415-778-6 (library bound)
  1. Québec (Province)—Juvenile literature. I. Title.
F1052.4.W45 2010
971.4—dc22
                                        2009027340

Printing   1   2   3   4   5   6   7   8   9

                                        PLB

CONTENTS

Quebec

Quebec City is the oldest fortified city in North America. Stone walls still surround the old part of the city that overlooks the St. Lawrence River.

A Mystery Student

Chapter

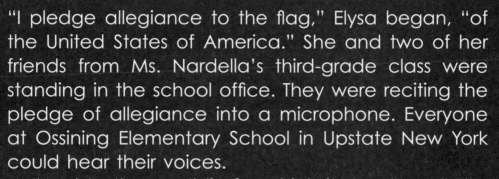

"I pledge allegiance to the flag," Elysa began, "of the United States of America." She and two of her friends from Ms. Nardella's third-grade class were standing in the school office. They were reciting the pledge of allegiance into a microphone. Everyone at Ossining Elementary School in Upstate New York could hear their voices.

"And to the republic for which it stands . . ." The words were so familiar to Elysa, she hardly ever thought about what they meant. But this morning, the words seemed extra important.

Yesterday, just before the last bell, Ms. Nardella had told the class that they were getting a new student from another country. She told them that the new student was a boy. But she didn't tell them *which* country he was from. "I'll give you three clues," she had said. She wrote them on the board:

QUÉBEC
QUEBEC

Sept-Îles
Port Cartier
Baie-Comeau
Rimouski
Chicoutimi
Rivière-du-Loup
Pohénégamook
St-Pamphille
Montmagny
St-Just-de-Bretenieres
St-Aurélie
Armstrong
Québec
Thetford Mines
Shawinigan
Victoriaville
Trois-Rivières
Richmond
Joliette
Sorel
Drummondville
Woburn
St-Jérôme
Sherbrooke
St-Hyacinthe
Lachute
Montreal
Rouyn-Noranda
Val d'Or
ONTARIO

Gulf of St. Lawrence
Golfe du Saint-Laurent
Gaspé
Cap-aux-Meules

St. Lawrence R. / Fl. Saint-Laurent

FACTS ABOUT QUEBEC

Total Area:
595,000 square miles
(1,541,000 square kilometers)

Population:
7,750,500 (2008 estimate)

Capital City: Quebec City

Monetary Unit: Canadian dollar

Ethnic Groups: Quebecois (or Francophones, Quebecers of French descent), Anglophones (Quebecers of British descent), and First Nations people

Religion: Roman Catholicism (unofficial)

Languages: French (official), English

Chief Exports: aluminum, airplanes, airplane parts, paper, copper, and alloys

Chief Industries: air-traffic control equipment, subway trains, helicopters, compact disks, software, air purifiers, and toys; space and aeronautics, pharmaceuticals, telecommunications, energy, transportation, and finance

1. His country is in North America.
2. Ice hockey is the national sport.
3. Many people from this country speak French.

When she was finished writing, Ms. Nardella turned back to the class. "Your homework tonight is to think about these clues and try to figure out which country our new student is from. You can use a map to help you."

Last night, Elysa had looked at a world map in a big **atlas** her family kept next to the dictionary and an encyclopedia (en-sy-kloh-PEE-dee-uh). She found North America. She found the United States of America. Two of the other countries in North America were Mexico and Canada. Since Canada is colder than Mexico, she thought it probably had more ice for playing hockey. The homework was easy, but it left her with many questions. And that morning, she had even more.

Elysa and her friends finished the Pledge of Allegiance and walked to their classroom. The rest of the class was already in their seats. The three clues were still on the board. Ms. Nardella was calling on students who had raised their hands.

"I think the new student must be from France," Rachel said. "People in France speak French." She sounded very sure of herself.

"But France is not in North America!" interrupted Julio. "France is in Europe!"

Chapter 1

"That's right, Julio," said Ms. Nardella, "France is in Europe, not in North America. Our new student is not from France. Which of the three clues is the most helpful?" she asked.

Elysa raised her hand. "Yes, Elysa?" Ms. Nardella said.

"There are three large countries in North America," explained Elysa. "The United States, Mexico, and Canada. The new student is from another country, so there's a good chance he's from either Canada or Mexico. The weather in Mexico is too hot to play ice hockey outside, even in the winter—so the new student is probably from Canada."

"Good thinking," complimented Ms. Nardella.

"But people in Canada speak English just like we do in the United States," said Jackson.

"Our new student is from Québec," said Ms. Nardella. She wrote the word on the board. Elysa noticed that there was a line, like a plane taking off, over the first e. She pronounced the word kay-BEK. "Québec is a **province** of Canada. A province is like a state. Most people in Québec speak French."

"And play ice hockey!" added Julio.

Elysa wondered what else was different about life in Québec.

"In English, we say the name KWUH-bek, and we don't use the **accent**," continued Ms. Nardella. "The new student's name is Jéremy." She wrote his name

Children in Quebec are excited when they figure out that they have ten days left before Christmas vacation—and they all wave ten fingers in the air. They study many of the same subjects as U.S. children do.

on the board, under *Québec*. "We will learn some things about Québec before Jéremy joins our class next week." Elysa noticed the same slanty line over the e in *Jéremy* as in *Québec*. She wanted to know what that meant, but she did not want to interrupt Ms. Nardella. There would be time to ask that, and many other questions, as they learned more about Quebec.

Quebec

Jacques Cartier put up a 30-foot cross of wood to claim "New France" for his king. His orders from the king of France were to discover lands with gold and other riches. The French thought they could sail across the Atlantic to Asia. Finding the American continent was a surprise.

From New France to
Quebec

Chapter

In some ways, the history of Quebec is like the history of the United States. Native people were living all across the Americas when European explorers first arrived. These early explorers were looking for a sea route from Europe to China. Instead, they stumbled on a "New World." People from Europe came to settle this new land.

In 1534, French explorer Jacques Cartier set foot on what is now the province of Quebec. He planted the royal flag of France in the ground and claimed the land for his king. He called it New France.

A year later, Cartier returned to New France. He was still looking for a way to get to China. If he failed at that, he hoped to find other riches, such as gold, in New France. He did find something valuable, but it was not made of gold. He found the St. Lawrence River. Cartier sailed to two native villages. These villages became the two biggest and most important cities in Quebec: Quebec City and Montreal.

Cartier did not find the sea route he was looking for. Nor did he find gold or other riches. He thought it was too cold and snowy in New France and did not want to stay. He returned to France, leaving no settlers behind.

Samuel de Champlain came to the village of Quebec in 1608. The name *Quebec* comes from a native word *kebec,* which means "where the waters narrow." Champlain wanted to build a French settlement at this narrow point on the St. Lawrence River.

Settlers came to New France for different reasons. Some hoped to become rich by trapping beavers and selling the fur, called pelts. Some were explorers. They wanted to map this new **territory** (TAYR-ih-tor-ee). Many were farmers. They came to make a new and better life for themselves and their families.

The settlers built walls to protect their trading posts and homes. By the 1700s, Quebec was a busy port. Today, visitors can see the old walls that still surround the old part of modern Quebec City.

While Quebec was the trading center of New France, Montreal began as its religious center. In 1642, a French ship full of settlers landed in Montreal. Many were missionaries. They wanted to pass their religion on to the native people. They built churches, hospitals, and schools.

Life in New France was very difficult for these early French-Canadian settlers. Winters were bitterly cold,

The French did not find gold or diamonds in Quebec, but they did find a source of riches. The fur trade was very profitable for France in the 1600s.

with a lot of snow. Surviving these natural challenges was hard. There were wars, too. At first, French settlers battled the Iroquois. The French settlers also fought against the British.

Both France and Britain were sending thousands of settlers to Canada. Wars between English and French colonies began in the 1600s and continued into the 1700s.

In 1690, British soldiers tried to take over Quebec City, but they were not successful. Bad weather helped the French settlers when the British attacked again, in 1711. Then, in 1759, British soldiers surrounded Quebec City. The strong walls protected the people inside, but no one could enter or leave. Trade stopped. It was impossible to bring in food. Finally, after a four-month **siege,** French troops left the city to fight the British.

The French were outnumbered by more than two to one. It was a bloody battle. Both the French commander, Louis-Joseph de Montcalm, and the British commander, James Wolfe, were killed.

The British won that battle. They took over Quebec City. A year later they controlled Montreal as well. In 1763, France surrendered its lands in Canada to the British. The French settlers were forced to live under British rule. Still, they were determined to keep their French identity and culture alive. This determination continues today among French-speaking people in Quebec.

The American Revolution (1775–1783)

The American Revolution spread to Quebec. More than 40,000 British settlers fled from American colonies to Quebec to escape the war. American troops attacked the British in Quebec City and Montreal. Some Americans, including Benjamin Franklin, tried to convince the French people of Quebec (who

Le Château Frontenac is a symbol of Quebec City. It was named after Governor Louis de Buade de Frontenac, who turned away the 1690 British attack on Quebec City. It has become the most photographed hotel in the world.

called themselves Quebecois [kay-beh-KWAH]) to fight with them against the British. It seemed to make sense. The French might finally be able to win their freedom from British rule. But the Quebecois refused. They did not want to be under British rule, but they did not want to be under American rule, either.

Quebec Becomes a Province

In 1791, the land that had once been New France was divided into two provinces, which became known as Quebec and Ontario. Mostly French-speaking people lived in Quebec. Mostly English-speaking people lived in Ontario. This helped the Quebecois keep their language and religion. However, they were still ruled by the British. They fought against the British for their independence, but they did not win their freedom.

Canada Is Born

The British North America Act of 1867 created the country of Canada as we know it today. Quebec, Ontario, and two other colonies—New Brunswick and Nova Scotia—were united as the **Dominion** (doh-MIN-yin) of Canada.

The new government of Canada was based on the British **parliamentary** (par-luh-MEN-tree) **system**. The people of each province elected their own government. The people also elected a central, **federal** government. The head of the Canadian government is the **prime minister**.

A Separate Quebec?

French **heritage** (HAYR-ih-tidj) sets Quebec apart from the other provinces and territories in Canada. It also makes Canada a **bilingual** (by-LING-wul) country with a rich culture. However, tensions

Provinces of Canada
July 1, 1867 to July 15, 1870

In 1867, the provinces of Quebec and Ontario were united with New Brunswick and Nova Scotia to form the Dominion of Canada. In 1870, Rupert's Land and the North-Western Territory joined Canada to become the North-West Territories.

between the French and British continue. The Quebecois have struggled to preserve French language and culture in Quebec. Some Quebecois would prefer to be separate from the rest of Canada. In the past, people have voted to remain part of Canada, but the issue is still not settled.

Quebec

Hot-air ballooning is a fun way to get a bird's-eye view of Quebec's farmland. Every summer, the International Balloon Festival of Saint-Jean-sur-Richelieu attracts 350,000 visitors, who watch as over 100 hot-air balloons take to the sky.

The Land and Climate of
Quebec

Chapter

Quebec is the largest province in Canada. It is located in the northeast corner of North America, and covers about 595,000 square miles. That's larger than many countries of the world.

Southern Quebec has warm summers and cold, snowy winters. In the north, winter temperatures drop below 0°F. Strong winds from the north blow from west to east. When these cold winds hit warmer air in southern Quebec, they cause a lot of rain and snow.

Long ago, the land was covered by **glaciers** (GLAY-shurs), which are slow-moving bodies of ice. The glaciers sliced through land. When they melted, water filled the valleys and holes. Now Quebec has great rivers and many lakes.

There are three main areas of Quebec: the Canadian Shield, the Appalachian Highlands, and the St. Lawrence Lowlands. Each of these areas has a unique landscape and special natural features.

Canadian Shield

The Canadian Shield is by far the largest of the three areas of Quebec. It covers most of the province. The Shield has many ponds and lakes, including Quebec's largest lake: Lake Mistassini. The land, however, is rocky. Only a small part of the shield can be farmed. Crops include potatoes and blueberries. There are also some **dairy farms**.

The shield extends far north into the Arctic, where it is too cold for trees to grow. This kind of cold, bare land is called **tundra**. South of the tundra are forests that are home to moose, bears, deer, raccoons, and many other animals.

Hundreds of thousands of caribou migrate across northern Quebec each year. Caribou are excellent swimmers. Hunting caribou is allowed in Quebec during certain times of the year.

The shield has important natural resources. Softwood forests are harvested to make paper. The Shield also has valuable **minerals**, including gold, silver, copper, and iron ore.

Long before Jacques Cartier first set eyes on Percé Rock (Pierced Rock), First Nations people fished in this area of the Gaspé Peninsula in eastern Quebec.

Appalachian Highlands

The Appalachian Mountain Range runs from Alabama in the United States into eastern Canada. The Appalachian Highlands area of Quebec includes the Gaspé Peninsula. The word *peninsula* means "almost an island." A peninsula is land that is almost surrounded by water. The Gaspé Peninsula is like a tongue that sticks out into the Gulf of St. Lawrence, which is a body of water between the St. Lawrence River and the Atlantic Ocean.

St. Lawrence Lowlands

The St. Lawrence Lowlands spread along both sides of the St. Lawrence River. This is the smallest of the three areas, but it has the most people. It includes Quebec's two largest cities: Montreal and Quebec. Nine out of ten Quebecois live in this part of the province.

This area is rich in natural resources. The fertile soil is excellent for farming. Quebec has many dairy farms that supply milk for making butter and cheese. Farmers grow oats and corn to feed their livestock. Other farms grow fruits and vegetables. The area is

Montreal is on an island near where the St. Lawrence and Ottawa Rivers meet. It is Canada's second largest city, after Toronto, which is in the province of Ontario.

also good for fishing, because the St. Lawrence River is full of freshwater fish.

As the name suggests, the lowlands are mostly flat and close to sea level. There are a few hills, though. Some are **dormant**, or sleeping, volcanoes. One of these, Mount Royal, is right in the middle of Montreal. It gives the city its name. Buildings creep up the sides of the hill. On top is a park.

St. Lawrence River

The St. Lawrence River is an important natural feature of Quebec, as well as one of the great rivers of the world. It links the Great Lakes and the Atlantic Ocean. Long ago, people traveled more by water than by land. The early explorers from Europe sailed up and down the St. Lawrence River. Native people called it "the road that walks."

Montreal is also the second-largest French-speaking city in the world, after Paris, France.

Basilica of Sainte-Anne de Beaupré is about 20 miles from Quebec City. Settlers built the first chapel on this site in 1658. Some people believe that the statue of Saint Anne inside the church can make miracles happen.

Life in
Quebec

Chapter

Life in Quebec is a lot like life in the United States, but French is the official language of Quebec. School subjects, such as math and science, are taught in French. Most Quebecois children speak French at home. They learn English at school as their second language. Although French-speaking people are in the majority, other groups also live in Quebec, including Anglophones (English-speaking people), First Nations people, and recent immigrants from other countries.

The motto of Quebec is *Je me souviens,* which is French for "I remember." People in Quebec know this motto well: It is on their

cars' license plates. But what exactly are they remembering? Oddly, this is a mystery!

The motto has its origins in the late 1800s when an architect named Eugène Étienne-Taché had

The design for the Parliament Building (L'Hôtel du Parlement) in Quebec City was inspired by the Louvre museum in Paris, France. The National Assembly of Quebec met in this building for the first time in 1886.

these three simple words carved under the coat of arms above the main entrance to the Parliament building in Quebec City. The architect never explained why he chose these words, and the true meaning of the phrase continues to be in doubt. Some believe this motto was the first line of a poem he was writing for another monument that was never built. Most interpret it as a reminder to reflect on their heritage, and to learn from history, both defeats and successes.

"First Nations" People

In Canada, Native Americans are known as "First Nations" people. There were three major groups of First Nations people living on the land when Cartier and Champlain came to what is now Quebec. They were the Algonquin, Iroquois, and Inuit.

The Iroquois became the enemies of the French settlers who began to arrive in the 1600s. Wars raged between the two groups, until a treaty was signed in 1701. The Inuit lived in the northern parts of Quebec. There are still Inuit villages in northern Quebec. The people do not live as their ancestors did. They lead modern lives, but they have kept some of their traditions.

Celebrating Winter

Southern Quebec, where most of the people live, gets a lot of snow. But the weather doesn't keep people indoors. The Quebec Winter Carnival and other festivals draw thousands of people to Quebec City, which is decorated with huge ice sculptures.

Freezing winter weather turns lakes into skating rinks, perfect for ice-skating and ice hockey. Ice hockey is the national sport of Canada. Children and adults play the sport. Families watch professional hockey games on television.

The Ice Hotel is like a palace made of ice and snow. A new one is built every winter. The rooms inside have furniture made of ice. Overnight visitors sleep in extra-warm sleeping bags on top of animal skins on beds made of ice.

Canadian Thanksgiving

Thanksgiving is a national holiday in Canada, as it is in the United States. Americans celebrate Thanksgiving on the fourth Thursday of November. Canadians celebrate Thanksgiving on the second Monday in October. English-speaking Canadians celebrate the holiday much as Americans do. Francophone (French-speaking) Quebecois may spend the holiday with family and friends, but without the traditional "harvest" meal of turkey and mashed potatoes.

Dogsled racing is a fun and exciting sport. Dogsled teams are usually made up of four to nine dogs. The most common dogsled breeds are huskies and malamutes.

St. Jean Baptiste (St. John the Baptist) Day is a national holiday in Quebec, celebrated on June 23 and 24. The holiday celebrates French-Canadian culture and includes traditional costumes and dancing.

Christmas in Quebec

Most Quebecois are Roman Catholic. Christmas is an important religious holiday as well as a time to enjoy good food and celebrate with family and friends. Families, even young children, go to **midnight mass** together. After this church service, instead of going home to sleep, families stay up and enjoy a long holiday dinner called Réveillon.

Quebec's winters are very cold. One fun thing for kids to do is play outdoor ice hockey. Ice hockey was born in Quebec. In the 1800s, British soldiers played hockey using sticks and balls. In the 1870s, university students in Montreal started playing the game using a wooden puck instead of a ball. They wrote the first set of rules for the game that became Quebec's national sport.

July 1 is Canada Day, a national holiday that celebrates the anniversary of the British North America Act in 1867, which united Canada into a single country. There are Canada Day parades and festivals with music and fireworks.

Bonhomme, which means "good man" in French, is the mascot for Quebec City's Winter Carnival. Bonhomme is short for Bonhomme de neige *(snowman).*

Céline Dion, Grammy Award–winning singer of such powerful melodies as "Beauty and the Beast" for Disney and "My Heart Will Go On" for the movie *Titanic*, was born in Charlemagne, Quebec. She's had hit albums in both French and English, and she has won many awards. She and her producer René Angélil were married in 1994 at Montreal's Notre Dame Basilica. Their wedding was celebrated throughout Canada.

Pierre Trudeau (1919–2000)

Pierre Trudeau was Canada's prime minister from 1968 to 1979 and again from 1980 to 1984. He supported French culture, and worked hard to make Canada officially bilingual. He did not support independence for Quebec. He believed that Quebec should remain part of Canada.

Trudeau was a **controversial** (kon-troh-VER-shul) leader. His beliefs made him very popular with some Canadians, and very unpopular with others. He was very smart, with an impish sense of humor. Once, when the queen of England was visiting Canada, Trudeau did a ballet twirl, called a pirouette, behind her back. Some people thought this was very funny. Others thought it was disrespectful.

Quebec

Jéremy knew it would be a big change moving from Quebec to New York—but at least he'd still get to enjoy the snow!

Bonjour, Jéremy!

Chapter 5

The morning that Jéremy was due to join their class, Ms. Nardella wrote some French words on the blackboard. Then she wrote what they meant in English.

"We have time for a short French lesson before Jéremy arrives," she said. "Repeat after me: *Bonjour.*"

"*Bonjour!*" the class said together loudly.

"Very nice," Ms. Nardella complimented the class. "Now, we all know that our new student's name is Jéremy. But he won't know our names. This is how

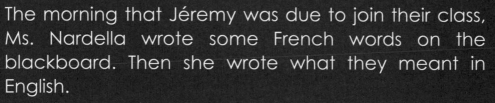

English	French
Hello or Good day	*Bonjour (bon-JOOR)*
My name is . . .	*Je m'appelle (juh mah-PEL)*
Please	*S'il vous plaît (seel voo PLAY)*
Excuse me/sorry	*Excusez-moi (ex-koo-zay-MWAH)*
How are you?	*Comment allez-vous? (KOH-mon TAH-lay VOO)*
You're welcome	*De rien (duh ree-EH)*

we tell him. I'll go first. *Je m'appelle Madame Nardella.*"

The students practiced introducing themselves: "*Je m'appelle Elysa.*"

"*Je m'appelle Julio.*"

"*Je m'appelle Rachel.*"

"*Je m'appelle Isabel.*"

There was a knock on the classroom door. The principal walked in, followed by the new student.

"*Bonjour, Jéremy!*" the class said together.

Jéremy smiled. "Hello, everyone," he said, with a smile. The classroom was decorated with maple leaf crafts the class had made in Jéremy's honor. The maple leaf is a symbol of Canada.

Jéremy took his seat between Elysa and George. Elysa saw he was holding a folder.

"I asked Jéremy to bring some photos," said Ms. Nardella. "This way we can learn a little more about him and life in Quebec." She walked over to Jéremy's desk, and he handed her the folder.

The class passed the photos around as Jéremy described how he grew up just outside Montreal. He spoke some English, but sometimes he used a French word, and Ms. Nardella translated it for the class. Elysa was impressed with her teacher. She had no idea that Ms. Nardella knew another language. Elysa decided that she wanted to learn French, too.

"How did you learn English?" Elysa asked.

Jéremy and his family go apple picking every autumn. Here he is with his parents, Josée and Martin, his baby sister Coralie (1 year old), and his older sister, Gabrielle (11 years old).

"We study English at school," Jéremy answered. "We also have classes for mathematics, art, science, music, geography, history, and . . ." He paused, then asked, *"L'education physique?"*

"Physical education," Elysa translated. She hoped she could learn to speak French as well as Jéremy spoke English.

"Did you have to wear a school uniform?" Rachel asked.

"Uniform?" Jéremy turned to Ms. Nardella.

"Costume." She translated the word into French for him.

"Merci," Jéremy said politely, and turned back to face the students. "No, I did not have to wear a . . . *oon-ee-form,*" he added.

"Do you play ice hockey?" asked Julio.

"I did when I was little," Jéremy answered. Elysa thought his French accent made even ordinary words like *little* sound special. "But I prefer soccer. It is my favorite sport."

"Mine, too!" agreed Julio.

Elysa had volunteered to make a special snack in Jéremy's honor. She brought out the chocolate sparklers that she had made. When she was looking up information about Quebec, she saw that these sparklers are special treats on patriotic holidays in Canada. They are especially popular on Canada Day.

Jéremy not only plays soccer, but he also likes driving his homemade go-cart.

Ice hockey may be the national sport of Canada, but soccer is also very popular. Here Jéremy, third from the right, poses with his soccer teammates.

The sparklers had been easy and fun to make— and they looked fabulous. She hoped everyone liked them.

"*Delicieux!*" Jéremy said after tasting one. Elysa didn't need a translation for that word. It sounded a lot like *delicious,* and the smile on Jéremy's face confirmed that she was right.

How To Make
Chocolate Sparklers

Ingredients

1 package (12 oz.) semisweet chocolate chips

1 tbsp. shortening

2 dozen pretzel rods

Rainbow sprinkles

Things You Will Need

Baking sheet

Aluminum foil

A large microwave-safe bowl

Spoon

Instructions

1. Line a baking sheet with aluminum foil.

2. In a large microwave-safe bowl, microwave the chocolate chips and shortening until melted, stirring once every minute.

3. Hold a pretzel rod by one end and dip it in the chocolate, leaving an inch or two uncovered. Gently shake the chocolate-dipped pretzel to remove extra chocolate, and place it on the baking sheet. While the chocolate is still wet, shake some rainbow sprinkles on the rod. Repeat with the rest of the chocolate and pretzels.

4. When all the pretzels are decorated, put them in the refrigerator for about 30 minutes, or until the chocolate sets.

How to Make a
Canadian Wind Sock

You Will Need

Glue

Scissors

String

Hole punch

**Red and white
crepe paper streamers**

**Cardboard
oatmeal box**

**Red and white
construction paper**

Wind socks show which way the wind is blowing. This wind sock is decorated with a maple leaf design, which is a symbol for Canada, and appears on the Canadian flag.

Instructions

1 Cut the round bottom off an oatmeal box so that you can look through it, like a big telescope.

2 Cover the box with white construction paper.

3 Cut out a maple leaf shape from red construction paper. Glue this on to the white part, in the middle.

4 Cut long strips of red and white crepe paper. Glue these "streamers" to the bottom of the wind sock.

5 Punch four holes near the edge of the other side of the wind sock. Cut two foot-long pieces of string. Thread each piece through two holes and tie them to make loops.

6 Tie one end of a longer piece of string to the loops. Tie the other end someplace outside where your wind sock can blow in the breeze.

Further Reading

Books

Costain, Meredith, and Paul Collins. *Welcome to Canada*. Philadelphia: Chelsea House Publishers, 2002.

Hamilton, Janice. *Quebec*. Ontario, Canada: Fitzhenry and Whiteside, 2002.

Kalman, Bobbie. *Canada the Culture*. New York: Crabtree Publishing Company, 2009.

Lackey, Jennifer. *Jacques Cartier: Exploring the St. Lawrence River*. New York: Crabtree Publishing Company, 2006.

Morganelli, Adrianna. *Samuel de Champlain: From New France to Cape Cod*. New York: Crabtree Publishing Company, 2005.

Works Consulted

This book is based on the author's personal experiences and contacts in Quebec, and on the following resources:

Bothwell, Robert. *Canada and Québec: One Country, Two Histories*. Vancouver, British Columbia: UBC Press, 1998.

———. *Penguin History of Canada*. New York: Penguin Global, 2008.

Brown, Craig (editor). *The Illustrated History of Canada*. Toronto, Ontario: Key Porter Books, 2007.

Bumsted, J. M. *A History of the Canadian Peoples*. New York: Oxford University Press, USA; (2nd edition), 2004.

Bumsted, J. M., and Len Kuffert (editors). *Interpreting Canada's Past: A Post-Confederation Reader*. New York: Oxford University Press, 2004.

Dickinson, John A. *A Short History of Québec*. Montreal, Quebec: McGill-Queen's University Press, 2008.

Ferguson, Will. *Canadian History for Dummies*. Hoboken, NJ: Wiley Publishing, 2005.

Riendeau, Roger E. *A Brief History of Canada*. New York: Facts on File, 1999.

On the Internet

Canada's First Peoples
http://firstpeoplesofcanada.com/fp_groups/fp_groups_overview.html

Defending Quebec, Capital of New France
http://www.pc.gc.ca/apprendre-learn/proj/d-q/index_e.asp

Exploration: The Fur Trade and Hudson's Bay Company
http://www.canadiana.org/hbc/intro_e.html

Further Reading

The International Balloon Festival of Saint-Jean-sur-Richelieu
    http://corpo.montgolfieres.com/en/general/salledepresse.asp
Quebec (Kidzone)
    http://www.kidzone.ws/geography/quebec/

Embassy

Embassy of Canada
501 Pennsylvania Avenue, NW
Washington, D.C. 20001
Tel.: (202) 682-1740
Fax: (202) 682-7726
E-Mail: enqserv@international.gc.ca
http://www.canadainternational.gc.ca

Canadian twenty dollars—
front (left); back (below)

Canadian coins: left to
right—25¢, $1, $2

Glossary

accent (AK-sent)—The way someone says words when speaking; a mark, such as the slant over a letter (é), that tells you how to say that letter.

atlas—A book of maps.

bilingual (by-LING-wul)—Involving two languages.

continent (KON-tih-nunt)—One of several large landmasses on earth.

controversial (kon-troh-VER-shul)—Causing strong disagreement.

dairy farm—A farm that raises cows for their milk.

dominion (doh-MIN-yin)—An area with its own government or ruler.

dormant (DOR-munt)—Not active; used to describe a volcano that is not erupting, but is not extinct and may erupt again.

federal (FEH-duh-rul)—Having to do with a country's central government.

glacier (GLAY-shur)—A large, slow-moving body of ice.

heritage (HAYR-ih-tidj)—A way of life that passes from grandparents to parents to children.

midnight mass—A Catholic church service held at midnight on Christmas Eve.

minerals (MIH-nuh-ruls)—Natural resources, such as metals, usually dug out of rocks or the ground.

parliamentary (par-luh-MEN-tree) **system**—A kind of democratic government found in England, Canada, Australia, New Zealand, and some other countries of the world. Representatives are called members of Parliament, and they are led by a prime minister.

prime minister—The head of government in a parliamentary system.

province (PRAH-vintz)—Part of a country, like a state.

siege (SEEJ)—An army strategy of surrounding a place and not letting anyone or anything (such as food and other supplies) in or out.

territory (TAYR-ih-tor-ee)—A large area of land; also, part of a country, like a state or province, with its own government.

tundra—Treeless plains of frozen ground near the North Pole.

Index

ABOUT THE AUTHOR

World traveler Ann Weil has written many books for children, including *Meet Our New Student from Australia*, *Meet Our New Student from Tanzania*, *Meet Our New Student from New Zealand*, and *Meet Our New Student from Malaysia* for Mitchell Lane Publishers. She loves Quebec for its food, people, and the opportunity to improve her French language skills. Her first visit to Quebec was many years ago when, as a teenager, she skied part of the *Coureur des Bois* cross-country ski marathon. Her 2008 visit to Quebec City included an overnight stay at the Ice Hotel, where this photo was taken. She also spent several days with Jéremy and his family near Montreal.